SPRING BOOKS

House Plants

House Plants

Text by J. Oplt

Illustrations by J. Kaplická

SPRING BOOKS

Translated by O. Vojtíšek
Graphic design by W. Ungerman

Designed and produced by
Artia for Spring Books

Published by
THE HAMLYN PUBLISHING GROUP LIMITED
London / New York / Sydney / Toronto
Hamlyn House, Feltham, Middlesex, England

© Artia 1968
Third Impression 1971
ISBN 0 600 01995 0
Printed in Czechoslovakia by TSNP Martin
3/01/06/51

Introduction

In this book the reader will find instructions for the cultivation and propagation of dozens of house plants which may be grown at home by amateurs. The selection of species comprises some unusual plants.

It is true that some of these plants are rather exacting and the cultivation of the more delicate species in some room conditions is difficult if not entirely impossible. On the other hand, given a thorough knowledge of the conditions of growth and development it is possible not only to keep most of these exacting plants at home but also to cultivate them successfully. In amateur grower's homes you may see magnificent specimens of rare decorative plants of which even an experienced professional grower could be proud.

With the present expansion of modern housing design there is an increasing number of amateur growers endeavouring to cultivate the prettiest or most unusual decorative plants, such as exotic species, which are in harmony with interior design in the modern home.

Basic information for the cultivation of decorative house plants

Before you begin to cultivate any plant at home it is necessary to become acquainted with many of the factors affecting its growth. These are the conditions under which the plant grows in its natural habitat. The requirements of plants as to the amount of light, humidity of both soil and air, temperature and nutrition result from these factors. Therefore select plants for which you can create, at home, the surroundings most similar to those they have in nature. A suitable selection of species is the first step for success in cultivating house plants. Some plant species live in the tropical rain forests; these plants must have an appropriate temperature and adequate moisture all the year round. In the case of plants growing in periodically dry, tropical regions, alternate the period of rest with the period of growth. If you do not rest the plants for a period, their living cycle will be disturbed, the plants will grow badly, will not flower, and eventually they might even die.

Plants of the desert, such as cacti and succulents, should be watered sparingly and given as much light as possible, and a poor soil. Too much water and nutritive substances are not good for these plants. In the text where the individual species are given, their natural home is described, and the cultivating conditions should be adapted to these requirements.

Light

Light is one of the basic factors in the life of a green plant. The necessary amount and intensity may be deduced from a knowledge of the surroundings from which the plant originates. An important factor is daylight — i.e. the allocation of light, determining the daily as well as annual rhythm of plants, their periods of rest, growth and formation of buds and blossoms. Plants are distinguished as long-day, short-day and indifferent ones. In the case of a long-day plant it is possible to accelerate the blossom formation by suitable additional light. The short-day plants are regulated, when necessary, by cutting down the available light. All factors affect the plants simultaneously; the lighting, however, has a great influence on the appearance of the plant, such as the colouring of leaves.

Water

Water is a second, but very important, condition of life. House plant requirements for the humidity of soil and air must be adapted to the conditions of the original habitat as well as to its daily and annual rhythm. In the rest period limit the watering but water thoroughly during the periods of growth, creation of buds and blossoms. Some tropical plants require moisture all the year round while the cacti which in their natural state live in a dry atmosphere require a dry soil, and will tolerate a dry atmosphere. Correct watering is the real measure of good cultivation. Apart from specific requirements of individual plants, several universal rules apply to watering.

The water requirements of plants change in relation to the age of the plant, the time of the day and the season of the year and the weather, light and temperature. With a decreasing temperature the plant's ability to take up water also decreases; with a low temperature and a surplus of water the roots and eventually the whole plant become damaged. With increasing temperature, evaporation increases and then the demand for water also rises. In a warm summer period, especially on sultry days, water the plants rather more so that they can retain a certain reserve. During a cold period when plants need less moisture they should be watered only enough to meet their immediate requirements. The temperature of the water should always be the same as the air temperature. Using warm water in a cold room is harmful, especially in winter, just the same as watering with cold water in a hot room.

Rain, brook, river or pond water are best for watering if known to have come from a clean source. Mains water is suitable for watering providing it does not contain too much chlorine. Well water is often the least suitable. In the case of hardy plants, however, great care in this respect is not necessary.

Temperature

A knowledge of the thermal optimum and the lower and upper temperature limits are very important in the cultivation of house plants. For the maintenance of correct temperature it is always necessary to consider the following factors: plant origin, temperature variations, the changing seasons and the age and condition of the plant. The temperature demands of house plants during the year may be shown by a curve on a graph, which rises following the winter rest period, reaching its maximum in June to August and then decreases again at the end of the year. In September to October development is usually completed and the period of rest begins. The course of the temperature curve during the day should always correspond to the temperature expectations under natural conditions, such as a temperature increase in the morning, maximum around noon, decreasing in the evening to an even lower temperature during the night.

The species recommended for cultivation in cool rooms require a winter temperature of 14—21°C (60—70°F), in air-conditioned homes approx. 10—14°C (50—60°F) and in warm flats 14—24°C (60—75°F). This classification, however, is only a rough guide, corresponding to natural conditions under which plants usually occur in nature. House temperature, however, should never be higher at night than during the day.

If correct temperature conditions are not maintained serious disturbances in plant metabolism are likely to occur.

Repotting house plants

It is necessary to repot house plants at certain intervals in order to replenish exhausted nutritive substances so that the plant does not suffer without them. It is sometimes also necessary to replant for other reasons, such as when the soil turns acid or when roots are unhealthy.

For most plants annual repotting is sufficient, although there are some which exhaust the nutrients in the soil so quickly that they must be replanted several times during a season. This applies especially to young plants. On the other hand, large, strong specimens of palms, oleanders and other decorative plants need not be replanted every year as long as continuous growth is apparent. An inspection of the roots is the best method to find out whether the plant requires repotting. If the pot appears to be a mass of roots, replanting is necessary. For repotting most plants, spring is the most suitable time, just before the beginning of growth. Replant into pots only a little larger than the previous ones, as in larger pots the soil easily becomes acid. If the roots are unhealthy it is necessary to remove the unhealthy parts and, according to the quantity of root, replant into the same size flower pots as those before repotting. If the roots are particularly damaged, replant into smaller flower pots.

A fresh flower pot must be thoroughly clean; a new pot which has not been used before, should be submerged for several hours in water before use. Earth for repotting must be fresh, well fertilized. Generally the rule applies that for plants of warm regions it is necessary to prepare a lighter mixture of soils, such as leaf-mould, peat and sand. Plants of cold regions, however, usually require a heavier mixture, e.g. mould, hot-house soil or turf with some sand. The composition of soil mixtures is given in the descriptions of individual plant species. For epiphytic plants, such as orchids, bromelias, anthurias, etc., use the following mixtures: roots of *Polypodium vulgare, Osmunda regalis, Sphagnum squarrosum,* beech leaves and charcoal. For terrestrial orchids add 1 part turf to this mixture (see tables).

A MIXTURE SUITABLE FOR ORCHIDS

	Osmunda regalis	*Polypodium vulgare*	*Sphagnum squarrosum*	Turf	Beech Leaf
epiphytes	1 part	1	1	—	$^1/_2$
epiphytes modern mixture	2	—	1	—	$^1/_2$
terrestrial species	1	1	2	1	—

A MIXTURE SUITABLE FOR BROMELIAS

	Semi-decayed beech-leaf	Rough peat	Charcoal	Rough sand	Turf
epiphytes	1 part	2	$^1/_2$	$^1/_2$	—
terrestrial species	—	2	—	$^1/_2$	1

11

All plants require a higher temperature after repotting so that they will take root quickly. Therefore do not cool repotted plants; keep them in closed rooms, spray them and water carefully. After repotting, the soil in the flower pot must not be too moist as the newly formed roots cannot absorb water so rapidly, the soil becomes acid and the roots decay. After repotting, when plants are sufficiently rooted and in full growth, they may be fertilized. In the shops you can obtain fertilizers with accurate instructions. It is advisable to fertilize with weak solutions and frequently. Never fertilize house plants during the period of vegetative rest or under low temperatures, or even plants that have been freshly replanted.

Propagation

Plant growers often want to grow new specimens of plants they particularly like. For most plants, the same or similar methods of propagation can be used.

There are some species which require propagating by a method characteristic for only those individual plants. Knowledge of propagation methods and the discovery of new ones is of great importance. Some species of decorative plants cannot be propagated, because the correct method of propagation is not yet known.

Decorative room plants are mostly propagated vegetatively, i.e. using parts other than seeds. It is obvious that the offspring will be in the same condition as the plant used for propagation.

In some cases, vegetative propagation depends on the season. Spring, however, is the best period for most plants.

The cuttings of many species root best in river sand, preferably roughly grained, not sieved. In practice the best results are achieved with a mixture of half coarse peat and half sand. The peat itself stimulates rooting. This method has the advantage that in transplanting the roots are more compact and take root more readily.

The preparation of propagators

With a small propagator it is possible to plant cuttings that are ordinarily difficult to root at home. As a propagator you can use either a glass frame made by yourself or an aquarium with a metal frame. Its size depends on the number of plants you wish to propagate. It is desirable to install an automatically controlled heating system in the bottom of the frame or aquarium. One of the best ways is to introduce into a copper tube of 1 cm diameter a spiral of resistance wire, covered with ceramic beads. This work, however, should only be carried out if you have a sufficient knowledge of electrical installations, or if you have someone who can advise you. As in this case the installation is introduced into humid conditions, then according to the present regulations a lowered voltage, e.g. 24 V must be used.

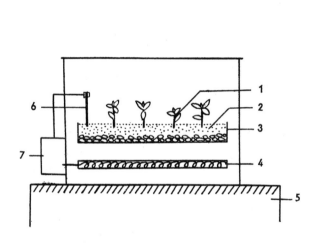

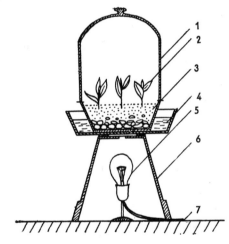

1 Iron aquarium of larger dimensions used as propagator

1. *cuttings,*
2. *substratum,*
3. *metal dish,*
4. *electrical heating,*
5. *stand,*
6. *contact thermometer,*
7. *relay*

2 Propagator heated by a bulb

1. *bell-glass,*
2. *cuttings,*
3. *dish with substratum,*
4. *dish with water,*
5. *bulb,*
6. *inverted flower pot,*
7. *stand*

3 Cuttings under a glass

4 Cuttings inserted round the sides of the pot strike best

About 5 cm above the heating element a dish of stainless steel sheet is placed on which is arranged first a 2 cm thick layer of pebbles, then an 8 cm thick layer of foundation, in which the cuttings are planted (see Fig. 1). The temperature is controlled by a thermostat, as prescribed for the particular species being rooted.

Another type of propagator consists of an electric bulb placed under an upturned flower pot. On this flower pot is placed a dish of water, and on top of that another dish with the foundation soil. The dish, with the cuttings planted in it, is then put under a glass cloche. For only a few cuttings a glass jam jar is quite adequate (see Fig. 3).

Some propagator designs are based on the experience that cuttings take best in consistently moist and well-aired surroundings. For example, the cuttings are put slanting into sand filling the space between two flower pots of different sizes, the larger pot has a well-drained bottom and the inner one is stoppered. The small pot is filled to about 1/5 with water. Water capillarity complements the moisture in the sand layer. The importance of this method should not be

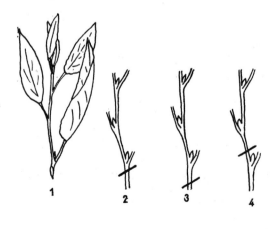

5 Stem cutting
1. *before treatment,*
2. *correctly cut,*
3. *cut too low,*
4. *cut too high*

14

underestimated, as it means that the young roots nearest the inner wall grow much the strongest, and cling tightly to the pot. The propagator should be kept closed until the cuttings begin to take root, and fresh air gradually let in when the plants become more sturdy. Well-rooted cuttings should be transferred into small flower pots and kept in a warm atmosphere.

Methods of propagation

Propagation by cuttings: A cutting is the stem, root or leaf of a plant which, after complete separation from the parent plant, takes root (under suitable conditions) and develops into an independent plant.

Propagation by green stem cuttings: Stem cuttings are shoots cut into sections. These are cut short, about 6—8 cm, with an inclined incision under the petiole (see Fig. 5). In the case of some species, such as *Ficus, Dieffenbachia, Codiaeum*, etc., the top cuttings should be cut longer, with 4 or 5 leaves. In order to make the most of the space in the propagator, it is necessary to roll lightly and bind the leaves. To prevent uprooting of the cuttings, each should be attached to a thin stick. The cuttings of plants that exude sap after cutting should be put into dry sand before planting. After the wound is dry, the plants are washed and planted immediately.

Propagation by leaf cuttings: Only species that have adventitious buds on the blade and leaf stalk can be propagated by leaf cuttings. The best known plant that propagates by leaf cuttings is *Begonia rex*, which produces adventitious buds on the whole surface of the blade as well as along the length of the petiole. Various species of *Saintpaulia, Peperomia, Cyperus, Sansevieria* and other succulent species are also propagated by leaf cuttings. (Fig. 6,7). The strongest plants are obtained when the whole leaf, with 1 or 2 cm of leaf stalk, is rooted. The leaves of *Sansevieria* are prepared for cuttings by cutting the leaf lengthwise in sections 6 to 8 cm long. Prepared leaf cuttings are planted in the propagator in the same way as stem cuttings.

Propagation by trunk cuttings: Many plants develop trunks relatively early and the lower leaves gradually fall off, leaving a scar with a visible bud embryo which, under certain conditions, may cause a new plant to grow. The scar stays permanently on the spot where the leaf has fallen off. This property is displayed, for example, in some species of the genus of *Dieffenbachia, Monstera, Philodendron, Dracaena* and *Cordyline*. When the plant is too old or ungainly the top part with green foliage can be cut off and planted directly into a flower pot, *(Monstera, Philodendron)*. The remaining trunks may be used for propagation. The trunk is cut so that every section has a bud and each cutting is put horizontally into the propagator. They take root in a short time and sprout a new stem. Rooted cuttings are then planted into flower pots (Fig. 8).

Propagation by tuft division: Some species of decorative room plants are propagated by the division of tufts in the spring, during replanting. Under favourable conditions, the plants grow rapidly into stout clusters. Strong plants may be divided into several parts. Each separated part must have a reasonable amount of root. In some species division by tearing is easy, in other species it is necessary to cut the tufts with a sharp knife. Plants thus separated are planted in suitably sized flower pots. Species of *Aspidistra, Asparagus, Cyperus, Clivia, Sansevieria*, etc., can be propagated by tuft division (Fig. 9).

Rooting by the lengthwise cut: The method of rooting by the lengthwise cut on the plant is usually only applied at home if you have no propagator and wish to achieve a limited success.

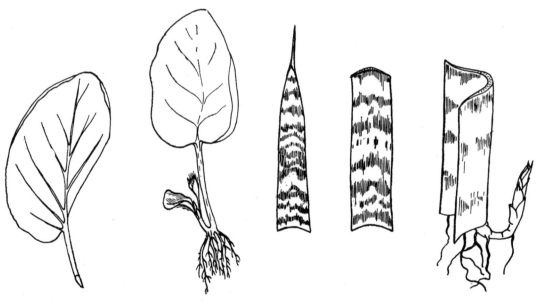

6 Leaf cutting of *Saintpaulia*   7 Leaf cutting of *Sansevieria*

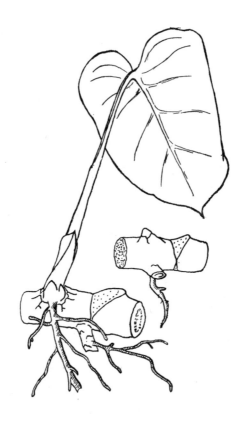

In the place where the plant should take root make a short cut under the petiole vertical to the axis and then lightly slanting upwards, as shown in Fig. 10. At the end of the cut surface put a piece of wood (a bit of matchstick) and fill in the split thus made with fresh moss, preferably *Sphagnum*. Cover the stem, over the cut, with the moss and bind with a soft wire. It is a good idea to moisten the moss packing and cover it with a polythene sheet so that the moss should not dry out and you need not moisten the packing constantly. This method of rooting may be used in the spring as well as the summer. The plant which has been cut should be put in the light near a closed window. In an approximate temperature of 20—22°C (64—67°F) lightly rooting species take root within a fortnight, harder rooting ones within a month. Rooting is sufficient when the roots break through the moss packing. Rooted sections are cut off and planted with the moss packing in reasonably large flower pots. After planting the young plants, keep them in a warm atmosphere in the early stages and then cultivate in the usual way.

The purpose of the lengthwise cut is the formation of a cutting on the plant. The interruption of approximately two thirds of the ducts in the stem directs a considerable part of the sap to the base of the stem-rooting part. Water transport

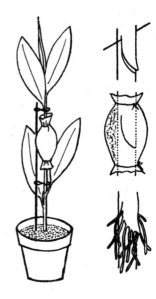

9 Propagation by tuft division

10 Rooting direct on the plant

from the root of the parent plant is not quite interrupted and therefore the rooted part does not die. The advantages of this method are that there is no need for a warm propagator, the rooted parts take root almost one hundred per cent, and natural warmth can be better utilized.

18

PLATES

Abutilon

Flowering Maple, Chinese Bellflower, Indian Maple

Abutilons are evergreen shrubs of the mallow family (*Malvaceae*) with 7-lobed palmate or elongated leaves, which may be multicoloured, with long stalks. They flower in winter as well as summer, depending on the species. They have well-shaped blossoms that are white or occasionally yellow and orange. About 100 species are native to the tropics and sub-tropics. The most frequently home-cultivated species are *A. thompsonii*, and *A. hybridum*, developed by the crossing of a number of South American species of this genus.

A. hybridum forms seed easily, but the young plants often have blossoms of different colours from those of the parent plant. If you wish to maintain certain colours, it is necessary to propagate vegetatively by taking cuttings. In the spring older plants should be cut down, so that they grow new shoots. The tops of the cut shoots can be prepared as new cuttings.

The blossoms and buds are removed, and the cuttings trimmed to a length of 3 inches; they are then planted in a dish with sand and covered with a glass jar in a bright warm place. After three weeks the cuttings take root and may be planted into 3-inch flower pots in an equal-part mixture of leaf-mould, turfy loam, peat and sand. After planting leave them some time by a window. In a week or so they can be replanted into 5- or 6-inch flower pots. In the summer place them in an open window on the southern side of the house and water them regularly.

If Abutilons are kept in a house where there is good light and a temperature of 10—13°C (50—55°F), they may blossom all through the winter. It is possible to keep them without blooming even with a temperature as low as 5°C (40°F). In the spring the plants are cut down and replanted. Large specimens may be put into wooden tubs. In the summer large plants may be placed outdoors and given plenty of air and sun; they will be covered with blossoms all through the summer.

Abutilon hybridum hort.

Acacia

Wattle, Mimosa

There are more than 500 species of *Acacia,* mostly native to Australia. These members of the Pea family *(Leguminosae)* are really trees or small shrubs. Fragrant Mimosa, a name often applied to the blossoming plants, is not strictly correct, since the true Mimosa is a related species known as the 'sensitive plant'.

There are not many Acacias suitable for indoor cultivation, but *A. armata,* a pygmy species, is often grown. It grows straight and has many branches bearing pinnate leaves about $3/4$ inch long. Blooming is in spring, with a profusion of simple yellow blossoms. Buds may appear as early as autumn.

If plants are to be propagated, they should be shaped by pruning in the spring following the flowering period. 3-inch cuttings are prepared from sturdy annual shoots and planted round the edge of a shallow tray containing an equal mixture of peat and sand. The tray is covered with a glass jar. If kept at a temperature of 15°C (60°F), the cuttings should take root within 3 weeks, when they can be transplanted into small pots of peaty soil near a closed window. After the plants have rooted in the new soil, cut off the tops to encourage branching. They should be transferred to larger pots (about 6") in the early summer, and both young and old plants should be kept in full sunlight through the summer, either in the garden, on a balcony, or by an open window.

Acacias should be wintered in a cold, light room at a temperature around 3—7°C (38—45°F). Moisture content of the soil should be carefully controlled all the year round. Acacias like moisture; they shed their leaves and die if the soil is too dry.

Acacias bloom from February to April, depending on room temperature. Young plants should be replanted in the spring after the flowering period, older ones after 2—3 years.

Acacia armata R. Br.

Aechmea

Grecian Urn

About 130 to 150 species of *Aechmea* are known. Some species are epiphytic; others are terrestrial. They are natives of Mexico, the West Indies and South America. About 46 species have been cultivated. These plants have markedly scalloped leaves, arranged in rosettes like their pineapple relations. Their blossoms generally form spikes, clusters or panicles.

Many of these species are regarded as very decorative perennial flowering plants. *Aechmea fasciata* is one of the most popular and most often cultivated. Others have variegated leaves. Their great differences in growth and colour of blossoms and of leaves make them very adaptable for decoration. Flowering, according to the species, is from summer to spring.

After flowering, and occasionally even earlier, two or more new shoots grow on the base of the plant. Do not separate them too early; they should be left for at least a year on the parent plant. Only when they are strong and well-rooted they should be separated and replanted.

Replant in the spring into the mixture for epiphytic Bromelias. Stronger growing species are cultivated as solitary plants in flower pots, the weaker ones on tree bark and in baskets. Aechmeas require a great deal of light, and should be placed in the brightest place in the house. In winter they are satisfied with a room temperature of 13°C (56°F) but the temperature should never drop below 10°C (50°F) on the coldest nights. Water them only moderately.

Aechmea fasciata Bak.

24

Aglaonema

Poison Dart

Aglaonemas are evergreen plants of the Arum family with thick stems that turn woody with age. They have oblong, brightly variegated leaves, which in some species grow near the base of the plant, and in others up to 18 inches high. There are about 40 species, all natives of Indonesia.

Aglaonemas are terrestrial plants, growing in evergreen rain forests. They adapt themselves very well to their surroundings in houses, however.

They are propagated by top cuttings and often as seeds. Spring is the most suitable time for propagation. Cut off the tops of older plants to include three or four leaves. Dip the cut surface of the new cuttings into charcoal powder and plant them in small flower pots with peat and sand mixture. Keep the pots in warm surroundings, or, if possible, in a warm propagator or a greenhouse. At a temperature of 19—22°C (67—72°F), the cuttings take root within a month.

The older plants from which the cuttings were taken continue to grow and soon become attractive specimens again.

The rooted top cuttings will soon need repotting in 5-inch flower pots. The planting mixture is composed of 2 parts leaf-mould, 2 parts peat and 1 part sand. Replanted plants are still kept in warm conditions. During the summer, if the plants are well-rooted, a weak liquid fertilizer should be added. Syringe the leaves once a day with clean water. Some species bear attractive red fruits, without artificial pollination, for quite a long time. At home Aglaonemas are cultivated both as solitary plants and in groups with other plants. They are ideal for window glass-houses or glazed frames, but the light must be controlled. In the home they should be kept away from the window as they cannot stand direct sunlight. In winter the temperature should not fall below 15°C (60°F) for any length of time. A slightly higher temperature does no harm.

Aglaonema treubii of Java

Ananas

Pineapple

The three species of Pineapple comprise a small genus of the *Bromeliaceae*. They are so closely related to each other that they are often taken as one species.

Pineapples originate in central Brazil and have for a long time been cultivated for their fruit. The Pineapple is a perennial plant that has a tough rootstock from which grows a rosette of stiff leaves. When the plant matures, a leafy stem approximately 18 inches high sprouts from the centre of the rosette, at the end of which a spiked inflorescence, composed of yellow bracts, is formed. The ovary forms only one fleshy fruit, and when this is mature a tuft of leaves grows on the top of it. In some parts of Brazil Pineapples can still be found growing wild even today. Over 100 cultivated varieties are known.

Ananas comosus fol. var. *variegatus,* has variegated leaves basically light green in colour, with white and red stripes round the border. It is often cultivated as a decorative house plant. Pineapples are propagated vegetatively by layering shoots, from the bottom of the plant as well as the top near the fruit. Separated small plants can be rooted in sand in a warm propagator. When the small plants are rooted they should first be planted into small flower pots (3½ inches). The best planting mixture for variegated Pineapples is 2 parts undecayed beech leaves, 2 parts coarse peat, 2 parts fern root and 1 part sand. Keep the plants very warm while they are taking root. They should then be replanted into larger flower pots.

Pineapple plants must be kept indoors all the year round in the sunniest place, but a humid atmosphere is essential in spring and summer. In winter they are satisfied with a temperature of 15°C (60°F) with limited watering, but should be exposed to full sunlight whenever possible.

Ananas sativus fol. var. *variegatus*

Anthurium

Tail Flower or Flamingo Flower

Anthuriums are upright plants, their thick stems sometimes forming a small trunk. Their leaves are heart-shaped, or lanceolate, often variegated. Some species are notable for the beauty of their leaves, others for strikingly coloured and long-lasting flower-like spathes enclosing the actual inflorescence. More than 200 species, mostly white or red, belonging to the Arum family (*Araceae*) grow in tropical America.

Some species, like the Flamingo Flower *(A. scherzerianum)* grow more successfully indoors than in glasshouses.

A bright position by a window, but not exposed to full sunshine, is best for Anthuriums. It is important to have a slightly humid atmosphere. During the winter these plants have a partial rest period, when they do not require much water, and the temperature should not be allowed to fall below 13°C (55°F). In summer they should be watered frequently, occasionally with a liquid fertilizer. After flowering, in spring, they should be replanted into a loose soil mixture; a good mixture is equal parts of cut *Sphagnum*, undecayed beech leaf, coarse peat, and sand. Good drainage is necessary. Some species will root quickly in moss packing. As a rule, Anthuriums are propagated by tuft division when they are replanted. Tops with roots can also be cut off and potted. In large-scale propagation, by florists, the plants are grown from seed.

Anthurium scherzerianum

Begonia

Begonia

Mostly plants with fleshy stems and alternate, simple or palmate-lobed leaves with long petioles, Begonias are sometimes epiphytic plants, though usually terrestrial. Approximately 800 species are native to tropical regions in Asia, Africa and parts of America. They have been cultivated, both indoors and out, since the end of the 18th century and their numerous species and hybrids are classified into tuberous, leafy and shrubby kinds.

Decorative Begonias are usually propagated vegetatively. Tall shrubby Begonias are propagated by top stem cuttings; the smaller species that do not grow a stem are propagated by leaf cuttings. Begonias may be propagated all the year round, but seem to do best in spring. Begonia cuttings easily succumb to a rotting infection and it is therefore necessary to observe absolute cleanliness. The dishes used must be properly sterilized. Clean coarse earth or equal parts sand and earth is the best foundation for propagation. Before planting wash the filled dishes with hot water, leaving them to cool before inserting the cuttings.

Top stem cuttings are trimmed to a length of about 3 inches, leaf cuttings are composed either of whole leaves or of leaf stalks about 11 inches long. It is also possible to cut whole leaves into sections and make cuttings from these. The cuttings are planted into a dish, covered with a sheet of glass or a jar, and placed by the window in a temperature of approximately 18°C (64°F). Cuttings of all species of Begonia root easily and quickly. After rooting plant them in 3-inch flower pots containing a mixture of 2 parts leaf-mould, 2 parts peat, and 1 part sand. Later on, in summer, they need to be replanted into larger flower pots.

In summer Begonias should be kept nearer the window but shaded from direct sun and watered when necessary. In winter the watering is cut down and the plants should be kept in a light place. House Begonias are very popular, with their attractive flowers and leaves and great variety of form. Although some species are rather exacting when it comes to their cultivation, there are a number of species that require only minimum attention to thrive in the home.

Begonia luzerne hort.

Bertolonia

Bertolonia

Originating in Brazil, the 9 species of Bertolonia are perennial dwarf plants with large ovate, entire or scalloped multicoloured leaves.

With their richly coloured leaves, Bertolonias are among the most attractive of tropical decorative plants. They need a humid atmosphere with sufficient warmth and moderate shade. As a decorative addition to window glass-houses and glazed frames, Bertolonias thrive and they are also suitable for use as a table setting. Some species, such as *B. marmorata* and *B. maculata*, can be propagated by seed as well as cuttings, but other species, like *B. houtteana*, although flowering, do not produce seeds and therefore can only be propagated by cuttings.

Seeds are sown in spring, usually in March, in a flat dish of clean, coarse peat. The seeds are sown thinly on a well-levelled surface; the dish is covered with glass and kept at a temperature of 18°C (65°F). The seedlings appear in about two weeks, when they should be replanted in a dish containing a mixture of 2 parts coarse peat, one part leaf-mould, one part cut *Sphagnum* and one part sand. Separated seedlings are still kept under glass. When they are strong enough plant them individually in 3-inch pots or in lots of three in 4-inch pots. Crock the pots well to make sure of good drainage, and place the pots in the window glass-house. When dealing with cuttings, the best mixture for rooting is equal parts of peat and sand, in a dish heated from underneath and covered with glass. At a minimum temperature of 19—22°C (67—72°F) the cuttings take root within three weeks. They can then be planted into the same mixture as seedlings. Bertolonias do not have a winter rest period and should be moderately watered even in winter, and the temperature kept at 16°C (65°F).

Bertolonia houttèana

34

Billbergia

Billbergia

The genus *Billbergia* of the Pineapple family is named after Gustaf Johannes Billberg, a Swedish botanist. There are 50 to 60 known species, natives of southern Mexico, Bolivia and northern Argentina. The plants are quite strong, mostly epiphytic with stiff spiny-edged leaves in rosettes. The inflorescence is formed of spikes with red floral bracts, often overhanging.

Billbergias should be replanted in spring or summer into the mixture suggested for epiphytic Bromelias. In replanting you may separate the stronger shoots, growing from the bottom of the plant. The size of flower pot is chosen according to the strength of roots.

For a short while after repotting Billbergias should be placed by a window. They require a great deal of light. It is not necessary to maintain uniform moisture content; on the contrary, periodic exposure to dry air often improves the colouring of the scales. The beautifully coloured inflorescence and floral bracts of Billbergias rapidly fade. There are some species however that have attractively coloured leaves which make up for the short life of the flower.

Billbergias are eminently suitable house plants as they will tolerate a very dry atmosphere. The most favourable temperature during the vegetative period is about 15°C (60°F), and in winter about 10°C (50°F). If the plants are kept in a cold room, it is necessary to decrease soil humidity. In this way their resistance is strengthened and they easily survive the critical winter period. Some Billbergia species, especially *B. nutans,* are quite adaptable, and it is often said that they are the most successful of house plants.

Billbergia saundersii Bull.

Bougainvillaea

Bougainvillea

Familiar plants of tropical areas, Bougainvilleas are climbing shrubs, partly thorny, with alternate simple leaves. They blossom on short side branches, the blooms are small but supported by three large cordate floral bracts coloured, according to species, rose, pink, violet, red, etc. One of the most popular is the Crimson Lake Plant, *B. glabra*.

Bougainvillea is propagated vegetatively by cuttings. At home the cuttings are best taken in June. These are the shoots that are still green and have not become hard and woody. The cuttings, about $2\,^1/_2$ inches long should be planted into a dish of sand. The planted dish is covered with a glass plate or jar and put by a window. The cuttings take root within a month, after which they are planted in $2^1/_2$-inch flower pots. Plant them carefully as they have very fragile roots. The planting mixture consists of 2 parts leaf-soil, 1 part turfy loam and 1 part sand. As soon as the cuttings take root they should be allowed plenty of fresh air. About the end of July plant them into 4-inch flower pots. After rooting water them well, and occasionally use a liquid fertilizer. Young plants winter at home near the window at a temperature of 7—9°C (45—48°F), with only little watering. In the second year the plants may be put outside in full sunshine for the summer. Adult shoots are trained up posts or trellises similarly to the *Hoya* or *Passiflora* species. Stronger plants need a period of rest, and during winter they have to be kept rather dry and at a low temperature. As the sun gains strength towards the end of February, begin watering again, and at the end of March they will begin to bloom. For brightly coloured floral bracts, put the plants by the window in the sunniest place. As Bougainvilleas are perennial shrubs, they grow year by year into ever stronger and more richly flowering plants. After the blossoming period replant and partially prune the plants so that new shoots grow.

Bougainvillea spectabilis var. *Crimson Lake* hort.

Camellia

Camellia

A striking feature of the lovely Camellias is their simple evergreen leaves — shiny, leathery and dark green. The beautiful flowers may grow singly or in clusters of up to three blooms in the leaf axils or on short stems. More than 40 species, members of the *Camelliaceae* family, are from India, Japan and China. The well-known *C. japonica* has a great number of varieties, some double-flowering, in different combinations of white, pink and red. Camellias are propagated from cuttings.

In February, March or August, cuttings about 3 inches long are planted in a propagator containing an equal mixture of peat and sand. For successful rooting, cover the cuttings with glass and heat from underneath to a temperature of about 24°C (75°C). After they have rooted replant the cuttings in small pots using a mixture of 2 parts peat, 1 part leaf-mould and 1 part sand. Both young and old plants need replanting in spring after flowering; very old plants need only be replanted every 2 to 4 years.

During the summer, Camellias can be put into the open provided they are shaded, either by an open north-facing window or in the garden under a tree. They need careful watering, with soft water, and will not tolerate soil too dry or too wet. In winter place them in the window of a light room, temperature about 5°C (40°F). Plants with buds must not be moved or carried about. On bright days it is often considered a good idea to spray the plants about midday, as they seem to do well in moist air, but the spraying should be stopped when the buds start to colour, and the plants watered round the base. Flowering plants can be placed in a heated room for short periods, but in general Camellias do not survive well at higher temperatures.

Camelia japonica var. *chandleri elegans* hort.

Cattleya

Cattleya Orchid

The familiar florists' Orchids are named after the English botanist W. Cattley. This genus of epiphytic Orchids contains about 40 species, natives of tropical America. The rootstock is large, and the stem swollen into a spindle-like, egg-shaped, or cylindrical tuber. The blooms vary from 2 to 10 inches in diameter and may be set individually or in clusters. Up to 20 blooms may be found on a single main stem.

The best temperatures for most *Cattleya* species are, in winter, 13°C (55°F) in the daytime, falling to 10°C (50°F) at night; in summer a daytime temperature of 18°C (65°F), 15°C (60°F) at night. The rest period of a number of species comes during autumn and winter, and at this time watering should be considerably cut down; a weekly check is enough to keep the plants sufficiently watered, and they should not be sprayed. As buds begin to appear, increase watering until the flowering period is over. Then it must be reduced again. Cattleya Orchids should be planted in the mixture given for epiphytes. Autumn and winter flowering species need replanting in March and April when the new roots begin to grow. Species that flower as late as June should be replanted when the flowers have faded. Tuft division can be carried out during replanting. After planting, water the plants once and then keep them rather dry until new roots appear. The new shoot begins to sprout from the bud of the last tuber, very soon after the new roots. During this period, water should be given more liberally; fresh air and shade are also necessary. Avoid annual replanting of Cattleyas.

If the developed tuber is given too much water, it will grow new shoots instead of blooms, so that watering needs to be limited. More light and air are also needed to ensure ripening of the tuber.

Cattleya labiata L.

Cissus

Kangaroo Vine

There are a wide variety of types of *Cissus* vines, some of them woody lianas, climbing with the aid of tendrils, and others more like shrubs. Some of the species form really large plants. There are over 300 species, native to the tropics, in the vine family. They are not related to English Ivy *(Hedera)*.

Cissus is propagated only by cuttings. The top cutting should be 4 inches long, while the remaining shoot is cut into sections with 2 or 3 leaves on each section. The cuttings are then planted in a propagator with a mixture of 2 parts peat and 1 part sand, and covered with a glass. At a temperature of 18°C (65°F) the cuttings will take root within three weeks, after which they should be planted into 3-inch flower pots. The planting mixture is composed of 2 parts leaf-soil, 2 parts turfy loam, 1 part peat and 1 part sand. Planted cuttings should be placed by a window at a temperature of between 15 and 18°C (60 and 65°F). Water the plants moderately in the early stages, and increase the watering after they have taken root. Smaller plants should be replanted every year during the spring and older plants after 2 or 3 years.

A number of *Cissus* species have recently been cultivated as decorative plants, as they can be used for a wide variety of decors. They are excellent as pot plants, shaped and planted out as single specimens, and can be used in groups from hanging baskets, etc. More sensitive species are only suitable for window glass-houses and glazed frames. A great advantage with some species is that they may be cultivated at home at a temperature as low as 4°C (40°F) and as high as 15°C (60°F). These species may be placed out of doors in summer. Other species have to be kept in the home in shaded conditions.

Cissus antarctica Vent.

Clivia

Kaffir Lily

There are three species of *Clivia,* natives of South Africa. They belong to the Amaryllis family and have tough, oblong leaves arranged in two rows, 2 to 3 inches wide and up to 20 inches long. Their roots are thick and fleshy. The stem ends in an umbel of 10 to 20 lily-like flowers.

Clivias are propagated by dividing their roots during February or, in large scale cultivation, sowing newly ripened seeds. Young plants are separated during replanting, which is usually done in spring, after the flowering period. To achieve blossoming plants as soon as possible after their separation, let them grow with the parent plant for at least a year before separating. To encourage your old plants to flower, replant them in a mixture of equal parts leaf-mould, peat, turfy loam and sand. The size of flower pot chosen for replanting is, of course, dependent on the abundance of the roots. It is always better to use a smaller flower pot rather than one that is too large. After replanting, water them a little. Clivias thrive in the home in half-shaded conditions, so they should not be placed right next to a window. During the summer, however, they may be put in a shady position in the garden. In summer the rooted plants should be well watered and occasionally given a suitable liquid fertilizer. In late September take the plants back into the house and reduce the watering. During the winter keep them at a temperature of 7—10°C (45—50°F). If the temperature is higher than this, they will blossom as early as December, and if lower, as late as spring. When buds appear, increase the watering. These plants often collect dust on their large leaves, so it is necessary to wash them from time to time. Clivias have not only beautiful blooms but also very decorative foliage. They make extremely good house plants.

Clivia miniata Rgl.

Codiaeum

Croton or South Sea Laurel

Codiaeum species are evergreen shrubs with brightly coloured variegated leaves. There are approximately 6 species originating in Indonesia and the Pacific Islands. They belong to the Spurge family.

Codiaeum variegatum from the East Indies is the most popular cultivated species, occurring in many forms with variegated leaves that are sometimes ornamentally twisted making them very decorative.

Croton is propagated by cuttings. Only the ripe, hard shoots are used; cuttings of the soft growing tops fade and fail to take root. Top cuttings should be trimmed to a length of 3 to 4 inches. The lower part of the shoot is then cut into sections with 3 or 4 leaves on each. The foundation for the propagator is made up of 3 parts coarse peat and 1 part sand. The propagator has to be covered with glass. Croton cuttings need base heating of at least 21°C (70°F) if they are to obtain a good rooting. After rooting, which takes about one month, plant the cuttings in 3-inch flower pots, in a mixture of 2 parts leaf-mould, 1 part peat and 1 part sand, and keep them in a warm place. Later on in summer replant them into larger pots. Croton is cultivated at home all the year round. Young plants thrive in a window glass-house where there is enough warmth and light. Older plants can be kept by a south-facing window. In summer keep them well watered, and spray the leaves. In winter they must be kept in rooms where the temperature does not fall below 13°C (55°F). They do not do well in the dry air of central heating.

Codiaeum variegatum hort.

Coelogyne

Coelogyne

Coelogynes are epiphytic Orchids, originating in the monsoon zone between Ceylon and the Samoa Islands. There are about 150 known species. They have bulbs with 1 to 2 evergreen leaves on creeping rhizomes. Their blossoms open either simultaneously or gradually according to the various species.

The white flowered *C. cristata*, a native of the Himalaya Mountains, is the most commonly kept house Orchid. From the aspect of cultivation it is not a difficult species, and beginners are rather fond of it.

Coelogynes should be replanted in March when the new roots begin to grow. The mixture for replanting is the same as that for epiphytic Orchids. Large shallow dishes are the best containers for replanting, as the plants grow in width. After replanting, place the plants by a window and water them moderately. Annual replanting is not necessary; it is sufficient to remove the old bulbs and to fill the gaps with new soil mixture.

During the growing period Coelogynes require fresh air and some shading. By the end of August the newly grown bulbs are already developed, and should be given less water and more air and light. During the winter period keep the plants rather dry at a temperature of 9—10°C (48—50°F). After the new floral buds develop, usually in January or February, begin to increase the watering. Place Coelogynes by a window where there is sufficient light. If it is a south-facing window, the plant should be shaded from the harsh midday sun by a light curtain.

Coelogyne cristata Ldl.

Cordyline

Club Palm

Cordylines are shrubs of the Lily family with sword-shaped leaves, forming a crown on a thin trunk, which is usually bulbous at its base. Approximately 20 species originate in Asia, Africa and Australia. In appearance Cordylines resemble Dracaenas.

Cordyline terminalis is one of the most beautiful species. In England, France and Italy numerous hybrids of this species have been developed, with maroon, red-white, yellow-green and other colours. These hybrids have not only attractively coloured foliage but also a delicately frosted appearance.

Cordylines are propagated in spring by cutting off the top of a plant with the leaves and trimming it as a cutting. The top cuttings are planted in small flower pots containing a mixture of peat and sand with an admixture of chopped *Sphagnum* and placed in a propagator with a bottom temperature of 21°C (70°F). They root well within three weeks. The remaining bare trunk of the parent plant can be cut into 2-inch sections to be planted with their bottom ends in the propagator. Even with trunk and root cuttings, reasonably good plants are often obtained. Rooted cuttings are then replanted into larger ($4^1/_2$-inch) pots, and in the spring of the next year into larger ones again. A suitable earth mixture for *Cordyline* consists of 2 parts fertilized leaf-mould, 1 part peat, and $1/_2$ part sand. Over the summer period occasional watering with a liquid fertilizer and frequent spraying, especially on sunny days, are advantageous. In summer they must be protected from direct sun; in winter they require a bright position. For good growth a summer temperature of 18—30°C (65—85°F) and a winter temperature of 13°C (55°F) is best. Cordylines with variegated foliage are among the most beautiful decorative plants. As house plants they grow fairly well. They do even better, however, in glazed frames and window glass-houses where the air temperature and humidity can be controlled.

Cordyline terminalis var. *tricolor* Kunth

Cryptanthus

Terrestrial Star

Cryptanthus is a genus of small epiphytic terrestrial members of the Pineapple family. More than 20 species are distributed in Brazil where they cover whole areas of forest land. These Bromelias have basal rosettes of delicately scalloped and usually variegated leaves. Tiny white flowers bloom in the centre of the rosette.

Cryptanthus is mostly propagated from the divisions that grow from the centre of the rosette after the blossoms have faded. It should be planted in groups of several specimens in small dishes or pots into a mixture for epiphytic Bromelias.

It is cultivated all through the year in warm, light conditions, and the winter temperature should never fall below 13°C (58°F), although this plant cannot tolerate direct sunlight. Care must be taken regarding the moisture content of the soil in summer as well as winter as the plant does not require a period of rest. Do not spray the leaves during watering as you might wash away its waxy scales. In summer an occasional watering with a weak solution of organic fertilizer is good for the plants.

In addition to the original species, there are a number of beautiful hybrids. Cryptanthuses are always very popular with amateur growers. They are suitable for planting on epiphytic branches and trunks, for setting up in displays. They do especially well in window glass-houses, glazed frames or terrariums where there is enough warmth and humidity. From the spraylike arrangement of their basal leaves, they are also known as Terrestrial Stars.

Cryptanthus bivittatus Beer

Cymbidium

Cymbidium Orchids

Cymbidium Orchids are epiphytic and partially terrestrial plants each with a short stem swelling into a flat bulb, with numerous sheathing leaves. The peduncle, which may be up to 40 inches long, carries 15 to 20 long-lasting blooms. More than 50 species are natives of the tropics and sub-tropics of Africa, Asia and Australia. The flowers, growing in long spikes, occur in a great variety of colours.

Cymbidiums flower near the end of winter and early spring. They should be replanted after the blossoms fade into the mixture suitable for terrestrial Orchids. Adult plants in large flower pots are not replanted annually. After replanting leave them for about 6 weeks in a room with little air circulation; later on, about the end of May, they will grow better if taken out of doors.

During summer they should be cultivated in a shaded position by an open window, on a balcony or, better still, in the garden under a tree. While the plants are growing they must not be allowed to get too dry. They grow better if they are sunk into peat or moss. During their growth water them often, and occasionally use a weak solution of an organic fertilizer.

By the end of August most plants have already developed ripe bulbs. When this happens gradually limit the watering till you cease watering altogether. In the autumn take the plants back into the house and leave them in a cool, bright, and dry position with the temperature at 7—10°C (45—50°F). Towards spring, with the help of warmth and light, buds appear on the plants. Begin to water them again at this stage. Strong plants create several floral stems or peduncles. For brightly-coloured blooms, artificial illumination is recommended.

Cymbidium hybridum hort.

Dendrobium

Dendrobium Orchids

Dendrobium plants are true epiphytic Orchids. They have a cane-like stem with segments either quite short and bulbous or slim and cylindrical, bearing deciduous as well as evergreen leaves. *Dendrobium* blossoms are sometimes solitary, or they may be distributed in twos along the whole length of the bulb-like stem, or occasionally in clusters crowning the stem. There are 900 species widely distributed in the tropics and sub-tropics from Ceylon up to the Samoa Islands, some species growing as far as north Japan.

Most species require high temperature and humidity during the growing period, and in the rest period dry and colder conditions. Only the tropical species have to be kept in rather warm surroundings during winter.

The growth period falls between March and August. Some warmth-loving species, such as *D. phalaenopsis,* do not begin growing again until May. The best time for replanting is shortly before the growth of new roots in March. They should be planted into the mixture suitable for epiphytes. Large plants can be put in wooden baskets, the smaller ones in flower pots. They do very well when attached to bark, covered with the planting mixture.

Dendrobiums should be placed on the sunny side of the house. Do not shade them in summer as indoors the sun is never likely to harm them. Water and spray the plants until the bulbous stems are properly developed.

The stems then ripen and harden, and leaves on the two-year-old stems become yellow and completely fall off. After this place them in a cool, dry, and airy place, at approximately 9°C (48°F). This stage is essential for the flowering of the plants, as it simulates the conditions of their native land. After a three- to four-month period of rest, small spherical bodies begin to appear on the stems. These are the foundations of blooms. At this time increase the temperature and water; they will then flower within six weeks. They propagate by means of small shoots that grow from the stems and take root.

Dendrobium nobile var. *sanderianum* hort.

Dracaena

Dragon Tree

Dracaenas are woody plants with a simple or forked trunk. Their leaves, which form a thick spiral, are narrow lanceolate, or sword-shaped. The genus is very similar to the related *Cordyline* genus. The more than 40 species are natives of the tropics and sub-tropics of Asia and Africa.

Dracaenas, especially those with variegated foliage, are important ornamental plants. They are much sturdier than Cordylines. In the home they are usually propagated in spring or early summer. Rooting straight on to the plant has proved to be the best method. Make a deep oblong cut in the woody stem of the plant (see Propagation in the Introduction). Pack *Sphagnum* moss all round the cut and cover it all with polythene; place the plant by a window; it will form roots within 5 to 6 weeks. When roots can be seen in the packing, cut off the top and insert it with the moss packing in a suitably large flower pot containing a mixture of equal parts leaf-soil, peat, loamy soil and sand. After cutting off the rooted top one or two shoots usually sprout from the top of the old plant. When they reach a length of about 6 inches, they should be cut off and planted as cuttings in a propagator. After planting, the rooted tops as well as the cuttings are placed by a window. In summer they should be planted in larger flower pots. Species with green foliage need less light than those with variegated leaves. In winter Dracaenas need a temperature of 13—15°C (55—60°F) with only moderate watering and rather dry air conditions. In summer, if the plants are well rooted, give them plenty of water.

Dracaena deremensis var. *bausei* hort.

60

Drosera

Sundew or Youth-wort

About 95 species of the amazing insect-eating *Drosera* family are known. They are found mainly in the southern hemisphere — in Brazil, Central America, south tropical Africa and Australia — but there are a few European species. All Droseras have numerous viscid glands on their leaf surfaces, which exude a sticky liquid. The fluid attracts small insects which become trapped in it, and are then slowly dissolved by substances released from the leaves, finally being absorbed. The plants are therefore termed carnivorous.

Only a few species, such as *D. capensis* and *D. spathulata,* are suitable for home cultivation. Seeds of these species are sown in the spring. The seeds are sown thinly on level peaty soil in a flat dish about 4 inches deep. The seeds should not be covered with soil, as they need plenty of light. A sheet of glass is placed over the dish, which is then placed in a larger dish of water. At a temperature of 13—15°C (55—60°F), the seeds will sprout within three weeks, and should then be exposed to full sun and air by a window. Two months after sowing, plant the seedlings out in fresh soil, using the same mixture. Use a small wooden fork for planting the seedlings, in twos or threes about 2 inches apart, and again place the dish into another dish of water that can be topped up when necessary. The first blooms of *D. capensis* begin to appear about five months after sowing. This species winters at a temperature of 7—10°C (45—50°F).

Droseras survive, when planted in this way, for two years, so it is best to start new seeds every third year.

These strange plants are interesting to observe, and particularly favoured by those with a taste for the unusual.

Drosera spathulata L.

Euphorbia

Spurge or Milkwort

Euphorbias are a large group of plants which vary greatly in appearance. Their leaves are simple, alternate and sometimes in whorls. There are also leafless types of *Euphorbia* with a spherical or pear-like shape.

The plant tissues contain glands producing a white milky juice, often poisonous. There are approximately 1,600 species, distributed all over the world with the exception of the arctic zone. One of the best known is the Beautiful Poinsettia *(E. pulcherrima)*.

The succulent species thrive best in houses. The beginning of summer is the best period for the propagation of these Euphorbias. Some species, such as *Euphorbia splendens,* should have their tops — approximately $2^1/_2$—$3^1/_2$ inches long — cut off at this period, to make them branch out. The cut off tops are used for propagation. When preparing cuttings, take care that the milky juice does not get into your eyes, or on your hands. After trimming the bottom ends, the cuttings should be put into finely ground charcoal powder and left in the fresh air. After two days, clean the cut surfaces to remove the solidified milky juice and plant the cuttings. The foundation for cuttings is prepared from equal parts of clean river sand and charcoal. As rooting is done in summer no bottom heating is necessary. Moisten the sand thoroughly and plant the cuttings by the rim of the flower pot. During the period of rooting do not use a spray, but shade the plants a little from intense sun, and keep the sand moist. Cuttings that have taken root should be planted in small flower pots. The earth for planting consists of 2 parts compost soil, 1 part turfy loam, 1 part peat and 1 part sand. It is useful to add crushed charcoal to the mixture. A good drain has to be put at the bottom of the flower pot to provide an outlet for water, as Euphorbias will not live in wet soil. After planting, place the pots in a sunny position where they will get plenty of fresh air. During the autumn slowly limit the watering, until a minimum level is reached in winter. Dry conditions do them far less harm than over-watering. The plants should winter in a sunny place, preferably at a temperature of 9—10°C (48—51°F). Replant them into fresh soil each spring.

Euphorbia splendens (Crown of Thorns)

Fatshedera

Fatshedera

Fatshedera is a hybrid of two different families, developed by Frères Lizé at Nantes in 1910. Its parent plant was *Fatsia japonica* var. *moseri,* pollinated by the Irish Ivy — *Hedera helix* var. *hibernica.* This hybrid is an evergreen plant, as are both its parents. It is a shrub with a thin straight trunk growing upwards at the beginning, and tending to continue at ground level.

Fatshedera is propagated exclusively by cuttings. Although it is possible to propagate it all the year round, it seems to do better before its growing period. The top cutting is prepared with three to four leaves and the rest of the shoot is cut into sections with one leaf on each. The cuttings should then be planted in a dish of sand. At a temperature of 13—18°C (58—64°F) they quickly take root. When they have rooted, plant the cuttings in small flower pots containing sandy compost soil. In summer transplant them into 5-inch pots and place them by an open window on the north side of the house. During growth these plants require watering regularly, and occasionally a weak fertilizing solution. *Fatshedera* is ideal for room decoration and corridors where there is only a little light, as it is a shade-loving plant. Older plants should be repotted annually in spring before the new growth begins. These plants must also be staked.

With its adaptability and modest requirements, *Fatshedera* deserves a greater popularity with cultivators than it normally gets.

Fatshedera lizei Guill.

66

Ficus

Rubber Plant

Among the *Ficus* plants, various types of growth are found; epiphytic climbing thin-branched lianas as well as straight shrubs and trees. More than 600 species originate in the tropics and sub-tropics, especially in India. *Ficus elastica,* the Rubber Plant, is probably the most popular.

Ficus species are usually propagated vegetatively, at a high temperature of 24—28°C (75—80°F) in the propagator. These conditions cannot usually be provided in houses, but you can use the method of rooting directly on the plant during the warmer months from June to August. Make a slanting upwards cut at least two-thirds up the stem (see the illustration in the Introduction on Rooting). Insert a stick between the cut surfaces so that they remain open. Then fill the space between the cut surfaces with wet moss and pack moss around the stem. Keep the moss packing constantly moist. After 4 to 5 weeks roots begin to break through the moss. Cut the rooted shoot off the parent plant and put it with the moss packing into a moistened flower pot (not too large). The planting mixture should be made up of equal parts peat, loamy soil and sand. Keep the new plants near a window until they take root in the flower pot. Later in summer place the plants by an open window and water them regularly.

Ficus plants do well even in the rather dry atmosphere of centrally heated rooms. During the winter place them in a bright position at a temperature of 9—10°C (48—50°F), or higher if possible. Adjust the watering according to the varying temperature. *Ficus* plants kept in houses should be transplanted during April and May at the beginning of the growing period. Young plants must be replanted every year, the older ones every 2 to 3 years. *Ficus* can be left outdoors in summer in the full sun. Through the summer they should be watered liberally, and brought back into the house about the middle of September.

Ficus elastica var. *alba variegata* Roxb.

Guzmania

Guzmania

There are 70 to 90 known species of *Guzmania,* natives of South America and the West Indies. They are terrestrial as well as epiphytic Bromelias with stiff leaves, forming a thick rosette. Their blossoms consist of clusters, spikes or latas. Floral bracts, in whose axils the blossoms grow, are often very attractively coloured.

Only a small number of *Guzmania* species are cultivated, as many grow very large and some are unattractive.

Guzmanias should be transplanted in spring or summer in the mixture for epiphytic Bromelias. They are propagated by division during repotting. The cultivation of *Guzmania* is similar to that of *Vriesea*. They are very exacting as to temperature and humidity, needing conditions of growth corresponding to those in their homeland. In winter, during the period of vegetative rest, they need a minimum temperature of 13°C (55°F), although the resting period is not essential. Through the summer during growth a temperature of 18—27°C (64—80°F), good shade, and higher air humidity are desirable. Take care when watering that the root packing does not become too wet.

Guzmanias may be cultivated successfully only in a window glass-house or a glazed frame where temperature and humidity can be controlled.

Guzmania intermedia hort.

70

Hedera

Ivy

The true Ivies are woody climbing plants with a thin stem bearing a large number of short rootlets or tendrils. The long-stalked leaves are arranged in a double row, with 3 to 5 lobes and very variable in shape and size. About 7 species originate in Europe and Asia.

The European *Hedera helix,* known as the Common or English Ivy, is cultivated in a number of forms. Over 150 varieties have been named, but there are many more, spontaneously arising as bud variations. They are very easy to propagate as cuttings. For house cultivation all the small-leaved and variegated types are suitable.

Hederas are propagated only from cuttings, which can be taken all the year round though spring and summer are really the best periods. Cuttings will form roots in water, or when planted directly into soil. Later varieties should be covered with glass after planting. Suitable soils for rooted cuttings are 4 parts compost with 1 part sand, or 1 part leaf-mould, 2 parts turfy loam and $1/_2$ part sand. They should be planted several to a pot.

Hederas grow in cool rooms, corridors, or even in north-facing windows. They can easily be trained to climb in various ways or used as bottle plants. In winter a temperature as low as 5°C (40°F) is tolerated. In summer they should be well watered, with occasional liquid fertilizer, but in winter less water is necessary.

If you are looking for a decorative plant requiring only minimum attention, it is likely that one of the varieties of *Hedera* will be suitable.

Hedera helix var. *goldherz* hort.

Hibiscus

Marsh Mallow, Rose Mallow

Mallows can be trees or shrubs, all with beautiful flowers. About 150 species are natives of the tropical and sub-tropical regions.

H. rosa-sinensis, originating in East India and China, is most suitable for cultivation in the house. It is a 4 ft high shrub, with lustrous green pointed scalloped leaves. The rosy-red blossoms are 4 to 5 inches in diameter; there are also numerous garden varieties in other colours. It flowers all through the summer up to September.

In spring older plants are cut down so that they grow new shoots. The top cutting is trimmed to about 3 inches in length, and the remainder cut into sections with two leaves on each. The cuttings are then planted in dishes of sand and covered with glass. If you intend to grow only a few cuttings, this is best done by making a lengthwise cut and packing with moss (see Introduction). The cuttings root within three weeks, when they can be planted in $3^1/_4$-inch flower pots, in a mixture of 2 parts leaf-mould, 1 part turfy loam and 1 part sand. After planting leave them in a warm position by a window. Later on they should be replanted in 5-inch flower pots and placed in full sun by the window. During the summer they grow well outdoors in a sheltered part of the garden. In summer they should be well watered, and a liquid fertilizer used once every week. These plants are propagated in spring, and begin to blossom as early as July. The blossoms fade fairly quickly, but as one flower is soon followed by another, the actual plants flower for a long time. Over the winter months place them by a window at a temperature of 10—13°C (50—55°F) and water them only moderately. This species is often considered as attractive as many Orchids. Even when not in flower it has decorative foliage.

Hibiscus rosa-sinensis L.

Hippeastrum

Equestrian Star, Amaryllis, Barbados Lily

Bulbous perennials with sword-shaped evergreen leaves and relatively large bell-like blossoms. About 60 species are natives of tropical America. *Hippeastrum* is generally wrongly named by cultivators as Amaryllis; this name really belongs to the South African plant, *Amaryllis belladonna*.

Hippeastrum is propagated by side bulbs or seeds that are sown immediately after ripening. The side bulbs, formed around the parental bulb, should be separated when they have produced their own roots. Old bulbs are transplanted after the blooms have faded, usually in March and April, in a mixture of 2 parts leaf-mould, 2 parts turfy loam and 1 part sand. The flower pot size depends on the size of the bulb. Between the bulb and the edge of the flower pot you should allow a gap of about one inch. The bulbs should be planted so that half of the bulb is above the soil. Small side bulbs are planted in 3-inch flower pots. After replanting place the plants in a bright and warm position by the window and water them moderately. In the middle of June they may be moved outdoors, either to a box of sand on a balcony or a flowerbed in the garden. The rooted plants should be watered once a week with a liquid fertilizer. From the middle of August gradually reduce watering, to cease altogether by October. After the leaves turn yellow and dry, clean the plants and place them in a warm dark room, without watering. Young separated bulbs are kept growing during the winter, and placed by a window moderately watered for the whole winter. Should a bud appear on the side of the bulb, place the plant in a warm light room and water again. When the first peduncles and blossoms begin to colour, place the plants in cooler surroundings, so that they should not flower too quickly. Repot the plants annually in spring after the end of the flowering period. Very strong bulbs, that get longer year by year, are usually cultivated in the home, so that by maintaining the proper conditions of growth and rest periods, their natural annual flowering is achieved.

Hippeastrum hybr. hort.

Hoya

Honey Plant or Wax Flower

Hoyas are climbing or trailing shrubs and sometimes epiphytes with thick ovate leaves and star-shaped blooms in umbels. About 200 species are natives of tropical Asia and Australia.

H. carnosa and *H. bella* Hook are the most popular varieties. *Hoya* is propagated by cuttings, and although it may be propagated all the year round spring seems to be the best period. Cuttings with one or two pairs of leaves are planted in a dish of sand and placed in a warm and light room where they take root. Rooted cuttings of *H. carnosa* are planted in 3-inch flower pots containing a mixture of 2 parts leaf-mould, 1 part turfy loam and $1/2$ part sand. H. *bella* is planted in a mixture suitable for epiphytes, consisting of 2 parts coarse leaf-mould, 1 part peat, $1/2$ part *Sphagnum*, $1/2$ part charcoal and $1/2$ part sand. This species should be planted three cuttings to a small flat dish or basket. It requires some shade during summer.

In summer replant *H. carnosa* in 5-inch flower pots. Cultivate them in sunny windows. Older plants may be kept outdoors. The shoots can be trained into various arched shapes. They blossom from May to November. After the plants have formed buds, it is not advisable to move them, as the change of light conditions may result in fading.

Both species are decorative, even when they do not flower, because of their lustrous foliage. They are well-known, proved species that often do better in homes than in a greenhouse.

Hoya carnosa fol. var. R. Br.

Jacobinia

Jacobinia

Plants or shrubs with large entire leaves, Jacobinias have one or more blooms in the axils of ornamental floral bracts and create terminal spikes or richly branched panicles. Approximately 30 species originate in tropical America.

J. magnifica is the most popular species for cultivation and has elongated tubular pink blossoms. It flowers between July and August. *J. pohliana*, sometimes also called *Justicia carnea*, with salmon-coloured blooms, is another favourite species.

Jacobinias are propagated vegetatively by nodal cuttings, usually in March. Plant the cuttings in a dish of sand and cover with glass or a jar. At a temperature of 15—18°C (60—65°F) the cuttings easily take root. Rooted cuttings are then planted in 3-inch flower pots, into a mixture consisting of equal parts leaf-mould, peat, loamy soil and sand. In the early stages, before they take, place them by a window. In May transplant them into 5-inch flower pots. For wider branching it is a good idea to cut off the tops once or twice in May or June. Place them by an open window in summer as they can take quite strong sunlight, and water them a great deal, but do not fertilize them with nitrogenous fertilizers as it diminishes the resistance of the plants. Cut off all the faded blooms. Jacobinias winter in the home in bright surroundings at a temperature of 13—15°C (54—58°F) with moderate watering. Jacobinias are very good window and room plants.

Jacobinia pohliana Benth.

Kalanchoe

Kalancho

Kalanchoes are succulents with fleshy, entire leaves and white, yellow, deep-red or scarlet blossoms in terminal panicles, composed of cymes. About 150 species are natives of tropical Asia and Africa. *Kalanchoe blossfeldiana* of Madagascar is the most commonly cultivated species.

If only a few plants are required they are usually propagated by cuttings; larger numbers are grown from seed.

In spring, after the faded blossoms have been cut off, the new shoots will soon begin to sprout. When the newly grown shoots are about 2 to $2^{1}/_{2}$ inches long cut them off and plant them into a dish of sand. The cuttings should be watered only when the sand is dry; try to keep the leaves dry. Plant the cuttings, three to a 3-inch flower pot, into a mixture of equal parts leaf-mould, turfy loam and sand, and place them by a window. When they have taken root and become strong, replant them into $4^{1}/_{2}$-inch flower pots. In summer keep them by an open window in the sun, and water them regularly. In August it is advisable to water them with a weak liquid fertilizer. Over winter put the plants in a light room with the temperature around 10°C (50°F); at lower temperatures their roots become affected with disease. Limit watering in winter so that the soil in the flower pots is only moderately damp. Increase the amount of water as the weather gets warmer. The plants bloom from January to April.

If you intend to develop the parent plant, cut off the faded parts after the flowering period and repot it; then treat it as those propagated by cuttings.

Kalanchoe blossfeldiana Poellm.

Lycaste

Lycaste

There are approximately 35 species of *Lycaste,* mostly epiphytic, some terrestrial, Orchids. They are natives of tropical and sub-tropical America.

The short egg-shaped bulbs bear one or sometimes three large, thin and deciduous leaves. The single blooms are on short peduncles (unsuitable for cutting and putting in vases) with several scale-like floral bracts, growing from the base of the bulb. Almost all species have fragrant blossoms. The 5 or 6 blooms are borne in spring.

They are replanted, after the blooms have faded, into a mixture for terrestrial Orchids with the addition of chopped beech leaves. After repotting place them in a room at a temperature of 13—18°C (55—65°F). Often older bulbs develop buds from which new bulbs begin to grow. The old bulbs must then be divided and the new plants propagated. During the period of growth, when they form many new roots, water them once a week and fertilize with a weak solution of organic fertilizer. During the growing period place them by a half-open window. After the end of vegetation and the maturing of the bulbs, which usually takes place in autumn, cease watering and put these plants in a fairly cool place at a temperature of 9—10°C (48—50°F). In spring, when the buds start to appear, begin watering again.

Lycaste aromatica Ldl.

Nepenthes

Pitcher Plant or Monkey-cup

Nepenthes are shrubs with long stems. They have leathery, lanceolate leaves, and the blade extends into a tendril shape carrying a multicoloured pitcher-like appendage with a fixed lid. Inside the pitcher a liquid, containing a digestive enzyme, is exuded. There are about 75 species of *Nepenthes* in the tropics, the greatest number being found in Borneo.

These well-known carnivorous plants catch insects and other small animals in their pitchers. The drowned bodies of insects then decompose in the liquid, and the plant absorbs the dissolved nutritive substances. The shape of the pitchers seems to be almost the same in all species; only the size and colour varies.

Both botanical species and hybrids are propagated by cuttings. New varieties are developed from seed. *Nepenthes* plants for house cultivation are usually bought at a florist as it is very difficult to propagate them at home. They should be kept in window glass-houses or glazed frames with other tropical plants. These plants are suspended so that the pitchers may develop. During the growing period spray the plants in the daytime, and occasionally water them with a weak organic liquid fertilizer. *Nepenthes* should be transplanted annually in the spring into a fresh mixture of 1 part *Sphagnum*, 1 part roots of *Polypodium* fern, 2 parts undecayed beech leaves, $\frac{1}{2}$ part pieces of charcoal and $\frac{1}{2}$ part sand.

Repot *Nepenthes* very carefully as the roots are very delicate. Replanting is done annually as, with the constant spraying, the compost in the flower pots becomes acid, and the plants are often affected by disease and die. Hard water should never be used. During summer they thrive at a temperature of approximately 27°C (80°F), in winter they should never be kept below 18°C (65°F)

Nepenthes mixta hort.

Odontoglossum

Odontoglossum

More than 100 species of *Odontoglossum* are native to the higher ranges of tropical America from Bolivia to Mexico. These epiphytic Orchids have egg-shaped or pear-shaped bulbs, with one or more leaves. Their panicles or clusters of blooms grow upright, occasionally overhanging.

New roots develop in the spring, and the plants can be replanted only at this time, never in summer. The mixture used is the same as that for epiphytic Orchids, with less *Sphagnum*, and the pots should be at least half filled with crocks. Use pots as small as possible. Repotted plants are kept fairly dry until the new roots appear in 2 or 3 weeks. From the end of May they like open, airy conditions in a north-facing window, shaded verandah or outside under a tree. Fertilizer need not be added, as the beech-leaf in the soil provides sufficient nitrogen.

New bulbs may develop in July and flowers occur in November, December or January according to species. Cut down the watering when the bulbs begin, and do not renew it until a flower bud appears on the last bulb. The time from development of the pedicel to the flowering period is about 6 weeks. Do not allow the blooms to fade completely before removing them, as this weakens the plant.

Some hybrids of *Odontoglossum* are considered to be among the best of decorative plants.

Odontoglossum grande Ldl.

Pandanus

Screw-pine

Screw-pines are branched trees and shrubs with numerous aerial roots. Their leaves are sheathed at the bottom, long, narrow, sword-shaped and sometimes curled, growing in 3 or 4 rows. *Pandanus* is often found growing along the coast. More than 140 species originate in tropical Asia, Africa and Australia.

Young plants develop on the main trunk of the plant under the leaves. If you propagate this plant, do not separate the shoots until they are well grown and beginning to grow roots; then plant them in small flower pots containing a mixture of peat, *Sphagnum* and sand. Propagate them in the spring; the plants need to be kept in a warm environment such as a window glass-house or, in summer, a room which receives full sunlight.

When they are rooted, repot them in a standard mixture of leaf-mould, turfy loam and sand in equal parts.

During the vegetative period occasionally water the rooted plants with a weak liquid fertilizer. During the winter period the temperature should not fall below 13°C (55°F) and watering should be somewhat limited.

The best position for older established plants is in bright sunshine. Older plants should be replanted every second or third year. Screw-pines are not, however, suitable for small flats, because as they grow bigger they take up too much space.

Pandanus veitchii hort.

Paphiopedilum

Lady's Slipper

Approximately 50 species of *Paphiopedilum* are natives of tropical and subtropical Asia. They are terrestrial evergreen Orchids. When young they have grooved leaves, bluish-green and sometimes marbled. Their large blooms are usually borne singly on a pedicel. They cannot live in extremely dry conditions during the vegetative rest period.

Their requirements regarding winter temperatures make it possible to divide them into three groups:

(a) 5—9°C (42—48°F) (b) 10—13°C (51—58°F) (c) 18—20°C (64—67°F)

Group (a): *P. insigne* and its varieties.

Group (b): *P. venustum, P. leanum, P. charlesworthii, P. lathamianum,* etc.

Group (c): *P. callosum, P. lawrenceanum, P. curtissi, P. mastersianum,* etc.

A knowledge of temperature requirements and partial periods of vegetative rest of individual species is of the utmost importance, and ignoring these conditions will result in plants flowering only occasionally or not at all.

Groups (a) and (b) are replanted in early summer, group (a) into the mixture for terrestrial Orchids and group (b) into a mixture for epiphytic Orchids. Group (c) transplant in any season into a mixture for epiphytic Orchids.

Strong plants should be replanted into large flower pots, weak or newly-divided plants in smaller ones. Fill the bottom part of the flower pot with crocks. After replanting do not water the plants too much, but spray them several times a day. After the new roots have formed, water normally and give them plenty of fresh air. If the plants are near a sunny window, shade them a little.

The species in groups (a) and (b) usually have new shoots by the end of August. Watering and spraying at this time should be gradually limited. Some watering can be resumed when the plants sprout new buds.

Warmth-loving species of group (c) should be kept constantly moist and warm as they do not need any vegetative rest.

Species in groups (a) and (b) grow well by a window, those in group (c) thrive in artificially heated glazed frames.

Paphiopedilum maudiae hort.

Peperomia

Peperomia

Peperomias are perennial evergreen plants, sometimes with creeping rhizomes. Their leaves are mainly fleshy, entire, alternate or in whorls; their blooms are not particularly decorative. More than 500 species originate in tropical South America.

Peperomias are very popular non-decorative plants. They are suitable for setting up in bowls as solitary specimens or in groups with other plants. Their modest humidity requirements enable their cultivation even in flats with central heating.

Peperomias can be grown from seed; they are usually propagated by cuttings, however. Some species, such as *P. magnoliaefolia, P. incana* and *P. scandens,* are propagated by stem cuttings, others, such as *P. hederaefolia, P. arifolia,* and *P. sandersii,* by leaf cuttings.

Stem cuttings should be $2^1/_2$ to $3^1/_2$ inches long, leaf cuttings with the leaf stalk about 2 inches long. The cuttings are planted in a dish of sand and placed in a warm and bright place. Peperomias take relatively quickly and easily. Rooted stem cuttings should be planted two or three to each 4-inch flower pot, leaf cuttings individually in 3-inch flower pots. After the roots have taken, repot them into 4-inch flower pots. The planting mixture is composed of 2 parts leaf-mould, 2 parts loamy soil, 1 part peat and 1 part sand. After replanting place the plants in a window and water sparingly. Give them more water only after rooting. The plants should be rooted before autumn. Winter them in a bright position near a window at a temperature of approximately 15°C (60°F). In wintertime water only a little.

Peperomia sandersii D. C.

Phalaenopsis

Butterfly Plant

More than 40 species of these epiphytic Orchids are distributed in Indonesia, the Philippine Islands and New Guinea. They have no bulbs, just a shortened stem bearing the blunt, ovate leaves, and blooms in straight clusters or panicles of large blossoms. Many beautiful hybrids have been developed.

Phalaenopsis is very exacting regarding temperature and humidity of the air, especially in the growing period. It grows well in window glass-houses, in which it is possible with artificial heating to maintain the appropriate temperature during bad frosts. Small plants are cultivated in flat dishes and stronger plants in wooden baskets. They should be replanted in spring before they begin to put on vegetation. Use the same mixture as for epiphytes but with a greater proportion of *Sphagnum*.

Repot them very carefully so that the roots are not damaged. If the roots adhere to the wood they must be cut out complete with the piece of wood. They often grow best when suspended. During the vegetative period they require a temperature of about 27°C (80°F), frequent spraying and suitable shading. In summer the rooted plants may be watered occasionally with a weak liquid organic fertilizer. If it is cold in summer then a little extra heating is necessary even at this time, successful cultivation depending very much on an even temperature.

Individual flowers bloom gradually and stay on the plant for quite a long time. Cut off the ripe blossoms, however, so that the plant is not exhausted. In winter through to March there is a partial period of rest, therefore limit watering and decrease the temperature to about 18°C (65°F).

Phalaenopsis amabilis Bl.

Philodendron

Philodendron

Approximately 200 species of *Philodendron* are known, all of them originating in tropical America. These interesting plants occur naturally as lianas or under shrubs, usually with a mass of long aerial roots. Some species grow as epiphytes in tree crowns. The leaves are often of very unusual shapes and different sizes. In tropical forests they grow under the crowns of trees, in shaded surroundings.

Almost all species of *Philodendron* are vegetatively propagated. Top cuttings are taken with two or three leaves, or trunk cuttings with one leaf. In case of top cuttings the aerial roots must be carefully arranged in the flower pots when the cuttings are planted. Trunk cuttings with one leaf should be planted, several to a small pot, in an equal mixture of leaf-mould, peat and sand.

Creepers, forming aerial roots under the leaves, propagate most quickly and may be planted several cuttings to a pot. Cuttings placed in a window glass-house or glazed frame at 19—21°C (67—70°F) take root quickly. It is possible to propagate them all the year round, but spring and summer are the best periods. For continued growth *Philodendron* needs the same conditions as it finds in nature, i.e. sufficient humidity, warmth and shade. In strong light the leaves take on a lighter colouring. Philodendrons should be cultivated in an equal mixture of leaf-mould, turfy loam, peat and sand. They are very suitable for hydropony (cultivation in sealed jars). Overhanging species can be cultivated as vase plants in brackets and on stands, the upright growing species as single specimens. They are very suitable for window glass-houses and glazed frames, and also grow in rooms without direct sun.

Philodendrons should be well watered in summer, and in winter, when the temperature is lower, just enough to prevent the root packing from becoming too dry. House temperature in winter should not fall below 13°C (55°F).

Philodendron imperialis Schott.

Pinguicula

Butterwort

Pinguiculas are perennial carnivorous plants with abundant roots and a rosette of entire basal leaves, thickly covered with stem-like glands along their top surface, some exuding a sticky secretion and others secreting enzymes. The sticky liquid traps insects, the enzymes decompose them and the resulting solution is absorbed into the leaf. The genus *Pinguicula* has 40 species, growing in muddy marshes nad peat-bogs on the mountains of the northern hemisphere and in the Andes. *P. caudata* and *P. gypsicola* are probably the best-known species for cultivation in houses. Both species should be grown in temperate conditions near the window in a terrarium with flower pots sunk in *Sphagnum*. The plants should be repotted in spring before they begin active growth. Stronger plants will often divide; they can be separated during replanting and each one treated individually. The best soil for repotting is a mixture of 2 parts coarse peat with 1 part of some limy substance such as old plaster. After replanting return the plants to the terrarium and cover it with a sheet of glass, raised on one side so that the air has access. During the summer place them between the windows in the half-shade, but in winter expose them to full light. Do not water the plants, just moisten the *Sphagnum* in which they are placed. Protect the leaves from water. *P. caudata* and *P. gypsicola* flower almost all winter. In spring, before the beginning of active growth some of the old leaves may be broken off for propagation. They take quickly and new plants are obtained that are replanted later on into flower pots. *Pinguicula* is also grown from seed. The seed is sown out on the surface of peat in small flower pots, and covered with glass. When the seedlings are a good size replant them in small pots and put them in the terrarium. On hot summer days tiny insects can be seen sticking onto the stem-like glands.

Pinguiculas are beautiful flowering plants, and their interesting habit makes their cultivation particularly rewarding.

Pinguicula caudata Schlecht

Piper

Pepper

Peppers are mostly climbing, evergreen shrubs. They have alternate, entire, occasionally three-lobed, leaves. The flowers have no decorative value. About 600 species are distributed throughout the tropical regions.

Peppers are generally cultivated as ampoule plants; they are very decorative. Coming from tropical forests they require warmth, humidity and shade.

They are propagated similarly to climbing Philodendrons and Scindapsuses. A whole shoot, together with a section of the stem and a bud is taken as a cutting. The cuttings are planted in a mixture of peat and sand in a dish, which is covered with glass and put in a warm place. When they have rooted plant them, three to a 4-inch flower pot in a mixture of 2 parts leaf-mould, 2 parts loamy soil, 1 part peat and 1 part sand.

At home they may be cultivated in window glass-houses and glazed frames, and are also suitable for large terraria. *Piper nigrum* may be cultivated as an unglazed ampoule plant. All *Piper* species are kept warm and watered all through the year as they do not have a rest period. If it is not possible to keep them at the appropriate temperature in winter (13—15°C or 58—61°F) keep the root packings rather dry.

Piper plants die at a temperature as low as 7°C (45°F), especially if the soil is too damp.

Piper ornatum N.E.Br.

Platycerium

Elk's Horn or Stag's Horn Fern

About 18 species of the *Platycerium* family are known; they are natives of the shady forests of Australia, tropical Africa and Madagascar, where they grow on tree trunks. They are epiphytic, heterophyllous ferns, the first leaves growing stunted, mostly with a rounded blade, adhering to the bark of their host. The stunted blade catches moisture and nutritive substances which fall from the crown of the host tree. These leaves dry up every year and remain on the plant, eventually being penetrated by their own roots so that the plant partly feeds on its own decayed parts. The other leaves are more normal, mostly forked and overhanging. There are patches of brown at the tips.

Like Orchids and Bromelias, Platyceriums live non-parasitically on the bark of trees. They penetrate the body of their host only when the bark is particularly decayed, and even then it is probably only in order to get a better foothold.

Do not transplant *Platycerium* annually; it is enough to add more soil mixture at the beginning of the vegetative period, packing it behind the blades of sterile leaves. *Platycerium* is cultivated either in shallow flower pots, on strong branches or hardwood, or on bark or cork. *Platycerium* is especially attractive planted in hollow branches, that can be made artificially of cork. Small plants sometimes develop from adventitious buds of older plants. When these plants have produced two or three leaves, cut them out, complete with the root packing, and plant them. The planting mixture should be made up of 2 parts undecayed beech leaves, 2 parts peat soaked in advance in manure, and 1 part sand.

Water them well in summer, and occasionally use a weak organic liquid fertilizer. In the vegetative period they need warmth, humid air and some shade. In winter a temperature of 13—15°C (55—61°F) is best.

In the house they can be suspended by a window or in a glazed verandah. Smaller plants are also suitable for window glass-houses or glazed frames.

Platycerium hillii Moore

104

Rhododendron

Azalea

Azaleas belong to the same group as Rhododendrons. They were previously considered a separate genus in the family *Ericaceae*. They are evergreen shrubs with alternate leaves grouped at the end of long shoots. Blossoms can be individual or set in clusters. There are about 350 species, mostly Asian but with a few native to Europe and America. Most Azaleas are outdoor shrubs, but *R. simsii (Azalea indica)* is a house plant.

Azaleas flower in the late winter and spring. They need a light, cool, atmosphere and will not survive in a centrally-heated flat. The root bedding must not become too dry; should this occur, the pot and base of the plant can be submerged in water and allowed to soak for several hours. Soft water, either rainwater or spring water, is suitable. Replanting is carried out after flowering is finished; the best soil mixture for replanting is coarse peat, forest soil and sand. Young plants need replanting annually, established plants only after several years.

In summer, Azaleas do well outdoors, preferably not in direct sunlight, and can be put in the garden under a tree with the pot sunk into the earth. If in constant sunshine, occasional spraying is a good idea, and the plants should in any case be well watered in summer; sometimes a liquid fertilizer is desirable. Before the light frosts begin, the plants should be brought back into a cool room. If Azaleas are cultivated in winter at a temperature of 7—11°C (45—50°F) in a good light, then they bloom from Christmas until late spring, according to variety.

Complete plants of Azalea should be bought, as they are not easy to propagate successfully at home.

Rhododendron indicum hort. (syn. *Azalea indica* SW.)

Rhoeo

Boat Lily

Rhoeo originated in Mexico. It is an upright plant on a short fleshy stem, with lanceolate pointed leaves, that are a lustrous olive-green on the surface and dark violet underneath. The diminutive white blossoms, growing from floral bracts, are not considered very attractive.

Rhoeo is easily propagated from top and side cuttings and sometimes from seed. The cuttings are planted in small pots of sandy leaf-mould. In spring place the cuttings in a propagator or window glass-house, and in summer move them near a window. The cuttings take root fairly quickly, and can then be replanted in 6-inch flower pots. *Rhoeo* blooms and forms seeds without artificial pollination. When the seeds ripen, it is a good idea to stand the parent plant in a larger dish of soil. The seeds fall in the lower dish and soon sprout. First plant the seedlings rather thickly, then repot them in small flower pots and later on into larger ones. *Rhoeo* should be planted in a mixture of loamy soil, leaf-mould and sand. In summer the well-established plants should be well watered, occasionally with a liquid fertilizer. In winter they need much less water. Occasional drying out of the root packing does the plant good. In winter it needs a bright position by a window at a temperature of 13°C (55°F), in summer it should be half shaded.

Rhoeo is an attractive decorative plant. At home it can be kept as a solitary specimen or in a group with other plants.

Rhoeo discolor var. *vittata* hort.

Rochea

Rochea

Succulent plants with attractive blooms, about 4 species of *Rochea* originate in South Africa. *R. coccinea*, also known under the name of *Crassula rubicunda*, is the best-known species. It has short decurrent leaves; older specimens become small shrubs up to 16 inches high. The flowers are crimson-red, grouped in a thick, flat cluster.

This species is propagated from cuttings, preferably in March or April. Make the cuttings about 2 inches long and plant them in a mixture of peat and sand. In a light place, at a temperature of 10—15°C (50—60°F), they rapidly take root. Rooted cuttings can be planted individually or with up to three specimens in each 3-inch flower pot, in a mixture of 2 parts compost soil, 2 parts leaf-mould and 1 part sand. Planted cuttings should be put in a bright position. In early June place them by an open window, in a small box of sand on a balcony, or in the garden, in full sunlight. By the end of June 'pinch' off the tops of the plants so that they branch out, and replant them in 5-inch pots. Increase the watering, and towards autumn occasionally feed with a weak solution of phosphorus fertilizer to help the development of blossoms. Before the frosts begin, place the plants in a cool room by a window where during winter the temperature may be allowed to fall to 3°C (37°F). Water very little in winter. With the longer days the plants begin to grow and form buds. Then it is necessary to increase watering. In April the first plants blossom and continue flowering during the whole of May. Rocheas are perennials so, after they have faded, do not remove them; cut them off, repot and cultivate as in the preceding year.

Rochea coccinea DC.

110

Saintpaulia

Usambra Violet (African Violet, Cape Violet)

Perennial plants, often almost without any stem, Saintpaulias are low, with a rosette of long-stalked, ovate, fleshy leaves. Their flowers have often only one bloom. About six species are natives of Africa.

A number of varieties of *Saintpaulia ionantha* have been developed. Rose and white blooms, derived from the original violet, and a double-blossom variety is also cultivated. Saintpaulias are propagated by seed and leaf cuttings. At home it is possible to cultivate a small number of plants by leaf cuttings. They can be propagated all the year round. Propagation from leaves is done using only vigorous, richly flowering plants.

Take a leaf cutting with a 3-inch leaf stalk and plant upright in a dish containing a mixture of peat and sand in equal parts. Planted pots should be thoroughly watered to begin with so that the soil remains moist for a considerable time and the leaves need not be sprinkled with water. At a bottom temperature of 18—19°C (64—67°F) the scions take root and young plants develop at the base of the leaf stalk. Rooted leaf cuttings are planted into 3-inch flower pots, in a mixture of 2 parts leaf-mould, 2 parts peat and $1/_2$ part sand. Place the planted cuttings in a warm room in half shade. As the plants grow, gradually transfer them to larger flower pots, first 3-inch and then 4-inch. During the summer keep them by a north-facing window, as direct sunlight turns the leaves yellow. Saintpaulias grow and bloom all the year round, so keep them at a temperature of 15—17°C (60—65°F) and water moderately in winter. Growth and flowering may be controlled by suitable nutritive solutions.

Saintpaulia ionantha Wendl.

112

Sansevieria

Sansevieria, Mother-in-Law's Tongue

Sansevierias are perennials with short thick rhizomes. There is a double row of sword-like leaves, fleshy and often decoratively striped. About 50 species are native to tropical Africa and India.

Sansevierias are vegetatively propagated; green-leaved species by leaf cuttings, variegated ones by tuft division.

Spring is the best period for propagation. Old, mature leaves are cut $2^1/_2$ inches long from the top downwards. Cut surfaces should be sprinkled thickly with charcoal powder. Plant the cuttings in shallow dishes containing a mixture of 1 part peat and 2 part sand. Variegated Sansevierias cannot be propagated by leaf cuttings as they would produce only green plants. Tuft division is the method used for variegated species. When transplanting in spring, cut off well-developed leaves with a part of rhizome. Cut surfaces should be sprinkled with charcoal powder. Plant the divisions in shallow pots with good drainage. After planting, keep them warm and water only moderately. Planting (of cuttings, divisions and standard repotting) must be carried out no later than July so that the plants are rooted before autumn. Choose pots that are only a little larger than the original ones as Sansevierias do not like to be in large pots. They should be kept in a bright position throughout the year. In winter water according to the house temperature; if it is lower than 18°C (55°F) no watering is advisable. In warm houses water only when the plant is really dry. Sansevierias are particularly suitable as house plants, as they grow especially well in the dry air of a centrally-heated house.

Sansevieria hahnii hort.

Scindapsus

Pathos

Scindapsids are lianas, climbing with the aid of numerous tendrils. Their leaves — sheath-like stalks — are shrubby and dark green, sometimes variegated, and heart-shaped. About 20 species are native to tropical Asia and East India.

Scindapsus may be propagated in any season; top cuttings should be taken with 2 or 3 developed leaves, and stem cuttings with one leaf only.

Plant 3 to 5 cuttings in one small flower pot in a mixture of peat and sand or leaf-mould and sand.

Planted cuttings must be kept in warmth and humidity. The cuttings take root very quickly and single-leaf stem cuttings sprout rapidly. After rooting, replant them in 4 or 5-inch flower pots. For the final repotting a nutritive leaf-soil with added sand is best. If the plants are well-rooted, water them with a liquid fertilizer. Fertilized plants produce large, well-coloured foliage.

Scindapsus should be cultivated at home at a temperature of 18°C (65°F), never below 13°C (55°F). In summer it does not like direct sun.

Scindapsus is a favourite pot-plant. Its popularity is partly due to its resistance and adaptability to house conditions. It can be cultivated as a climber or upright on moss trunks. At home *Scindapsus* may be grown on walls even where there is no sunlight. Suitable for window glass-houses, etc; cultivation in sealed glass jars has also given good results. It often takes the place of the more demanding *Tradescantia* in the home.

Scindapsus pictus Engler.

Stapelia

Stapelia, Starfish Flower, Toad Flower, Carrion Flower

Stapelias are stem-like leafless succulent plants, with quadrangular stems about 1 foot long and $1/_2$ inch thick. The flowers have an unpleasant smell and grow individually or sometimes a group.

In a vegetative state Stapelias are not as attractive as some other succulent plants, but they excel in their dramatic blossoms.

Stapelias are propagated vegetatively as well as from seed. In spring during transplanting, separate the weaker stems (grown during the last year) from the parent plant and plant them several to a $3^1/_2$-inch pot. Crock one third of the pot. The planting mixture is composed of 2 parts leaf-mould, 1 part turfy loam, $1/_2$ part charcoal and $1/_2$ part sand. The next year replant them into flat dishes so that new stems can be formed for flowering. In summer keep them between windows in full sunshine and water them well. Towards autumn when the stems are completing their growth cut the watering, but do not stop watering completely. Overdried roots wither and lose their ability to absorb water, when they easily decay and the whole plant might die. In winter keep the plants in a bright position with other succulents at a temperature of 9°C (48°F) and water them much less. Stapelias should be repotted between April and May. Take care only to select plants with new stems on which they will flower.

Stapelia variegata L.

Tillandsia

Tillandsia, Old Man's Beard, Spanish Moss

Tillandsias are mostly epiphytic Bromelias with narrow, sheathed leaves, growing in very different shapes and ways. The flowers grow at the end of a long stem. The size of blooms varies a great deal; their colour also varies, sometimes blue, violet, yellow, green to yellow-green, but rarely red. The genus *Tillandsia* was named by Linné after the Finish professor, Elias Tillands. More than 400 species are natives of South America. As epiphytic plants, Tillandsias are adapted to harder living conditions and they are therefore very suitable for indoor cultivation. According to their living conditions they are divided into two groups.

The first group consists of epiphytes growing in humus such as decayed leaves, wood, etc., deposited in the forks of trees. These are cultivated in exactly the same way as *Vriesia*. The second group is formed by epiphytes directly growing on the bark of trees; these conserve moisture through a scale-like arrangement of the basal leaves and can survive particularly difficult living conditions. These species are only cultivated on rough branches or strong roots. The base of the plant must be covered with bits of root, fern and *Sphagnum* and fitted by a stainless wire to the branch. Branches planted like this are suspended in window glass-houses. It does the plants good for the compost occasionally to dry out before being moistened again, as happens in nature. If possible use rain water for watering, and occasionally supply a weak organic liquid fertilizer. Keep the winter temperature at 10—12°C (50—55°F) with limited watering. Their small size allows cultivation of more plants in a limited space, and their way of life and interesting appearance make them very popular with growers.

Tillandsia juncea Lecq.

120

Vallota

Vallota, Scarborough Lily

Vallota purpurea originates in South Africa. It has a brown egg-shaped bulb bearing elongated leaves, 1 to 1½ inches wide and 12 to 16 inches long. The main stem grows from the centre of the leaves, and is about 10 inches high, ending in an umbel of flowers.

More robust plants have several peduncles. Blossoms are fiery vermilion and may be up to 3½ inches across. They are now rarely cultivated by florists. They once used to be one of the best known house plants.

Vallota is propagated from seeds and side-bulbs. The plants propagated by side bulbs mature faster. Small plants are formed on both sides of the bulb. After sprouting leaflets and forming its own roots, the small bulb remains joined to the parent bulb; they should be divided in good time before the parent plants weaken. Separated bulbs should be planted two to a 3-inch flower pot in a mixture of 2 parts leaf-mould, 2 parts turfy loam and 1 part sand, and placed in a bright position by a window. During the winter *Vallota* does not have a complete period of vegetative rest; it needs some watering and a temperature of 7°—10°C (45—50°F). Old and young plants should be repotted in April. Keep them all year by a window in a bright position. During summer they may stay by an open window, but require a great deal of watering and occasionally a fertilizing solution. In August, decrease the watering, and in September the plants will flower. With good cultivation stronger bulbs, developed from side-bulbs, flower in the third year. Well-established bulbs often flower annually.

Vallota purpurea Herb.

Vanda

Vanda

Vanda is an interesting genus of epiphytic Orchids. There are more than 50 species, natives of the monsoon region between India and New Guinea. The stem is stout, upright and thickly covered with two rows of leathery leaves, whose axils hold large clusters of blooms.

These Orchids should be replanted every few years. The strong aerial roots, growing horizontally when young, must be tied to the main stem so that they grow downwards. Vandas are replanted after the flowers fade, usually in March or April, into the mixture for epiphytes. With tall specimens, cut off the strong tops with well-developed roots and pot them separately. The size of the flower pot depends on the strength of the plant and its roots. Put plenty of croks in the bottom of the pot and pack down compost firmly between them. After replanting they require more warmth and humidity, but no leaf-spraying. If the plants are kept by a window, they should be shaded. They grow from March to August, and after September the plants should be left dry and hardened by airing. In autumn and winter the temperature may be allowed to fall to 10—13°C (50—55°F).

Some species, such as *V. coerulea,* begin to blossom in December, and retarded specimens as late as January or February. These species must be kept warmer and moderately watered. Other species flower as late as March or April. At that time the root tips renew their growth. After the flowers have faded a new period of growth takes place.

If kept in suitable conditions, Vandas should flower annually.

Vanda tricolor Lem.

Vriesea

Vriesia

The species *Vriesea* are mostly epiphytic herbs. They have a shortened stem with a rosette of bare, large, soft green leaves that are often marbled. In the axils of large, usually variegated floral bracts, yellow or greenish blooms grow, forming large beautiful spikes on leafless stems. There are more than 100 species in South and Central America. The genus was named after the Dutch botanist, W. H. de Vries.

Species with variegated foliage are striking even when not in flower. The roots of Vriesias are only weakly developed and serve as anchoring organs. It was once assumed that the roots had no absorptive power, but in a manured foundation or if treated with a liquid fertilizer they do grow much more luxuriantly.

The plants of this genus have no period of vegetative rest. But conditions for constant growth can only be provided in a window glass-house where it is possible to control temperature and moisture.

Vriesias have to be replanted in spring or summer in a foundation for epiphytic Bromelias. Plant firmly as the crumbling of loose soil uproots them. Bearing in mind that the root system is negligible, plant as far as possible in small pots, choosing the pots according to the size of the plant and its root packing. After repotting increase the temperature. Vriesias do not provide many divisions, usually only one or two after the flowers have faded. If new plants have already grown from the division, cut off the old faded parts. During the summer they require half-shade. They are as attractive as solitary specimens as they are when planted on epiphytic trunks or branches.

Green-leaved species winter at about 13°C (55°F); the variegated ones, belonging to the group *V. splendens*, need a higher temperature of 15—18°C (60—65°F).

Vriesea splendens Lem.

Zebrina

Zebrina

Zebrinas are perennial plants with a creeping stem and clasping pointed ovate leaves, purple underneath, green on the surface, with silvery stripes. Red species originating in Mexico are also known.

Zebrinas are easily propagated by stem cuttings like Tradescantias. Zebrina cuttings should not be rooted separately in a propagator but planted after preparation, 8 to 10 cuttings in each 5-inch flowerpot. In a short time attractive plants begin to grow. Gardening soil and sand is the most suitable medium. In over-rich soil and with too much moisture the colour fades. Although Zebrina is a marshy plant with fleshy stems, it keeps for several months without soil and water if cut off and loosely suspended in the air.

Zebrinas are very suitable for glass containers of water, hung on walls. Before a cutting is put in water the leaves must be removed from the lower stem. Zebrinas are useful for adding to plants that have already been in large and old vessels as they soon spread and may hide an ugly appearance. If you place Zebrinas at home in a bright position by a window, they will grow into attractive ornamental plants. During the summer they may be kept without flower pots in wooden boxes on a balcony or in a garden. In autumn cut off the tops and pot them again. Zebrinas will also grow well in rather dry surroundings. During winter keep them in a bright place at a temperature of 10—13°C (50—55°F).

Zebrina pendula var. *quadricolor* hort.

Zygocactus

Christmas Cactus

Zygocacti are recognized by their flat stem segments. In their natural habitat they usually grow on trees, forming a short trunk with overhanging branches. Flowers form at the end of the stem segments. Only about 5 species are known, mostly originating in Brazil.

Zygocactus is propagated vegetatively by cuttings and grafting. Spring is the most suitable period for propagation. Cuttings with two segments are then prepared and planted in dishes of sand. Rooted cuttings are replanted into 3-inch flower pots in an equal mixture of earth, leaf-mould, peat, loamy soil and sand. Place them in a window and water moderately at first. In summer they may be placed in the sun by an open window and watered more often. At the beginning of September watering must be limited so that the segments can ripen and produce blossoms. Plants that are constantly watered do not flower well. *Zygocactus* should be replanted in March, taking into consideration the size of the roots in selecting suitable pots.

In winter a temperature of 10—13°C (50—55°F) suits them best. When buds appear increase the watering slightly. To obtain luxuriant plants with overhanging crowns, graft *Zygocactus* on the robustly growing *Peireskia* species. The shoots are kept in a warm room, start to sprout in March, and are then grafted onto the stock. The slip is taken with two segments. Grafted plants should be covered for three weeks with a tall glass jar. At room temperature the slip and stock continue to grow together, then during the summer they will form a branched crown.

Zygocacti are very ornamental plants. Their greatest attraction is that they have brightly-coloured blossoms and flower in the winter when there are few other flowering plants.

Zygocactus truncatus K. SCH. (Syn. *Epiphyllum truncatum* Haw.)

INDEX